Improve Your Social Confidence

How to Eliminate Your Insecurities, Social Anxiety and Shyness

Disclaimer

All attempts have been made to verify the information in this book; however, neither the author nor the publisher assumes any responsibility for errors, omissions, or contrary interpretations of the content within.

This book is for entertainment purposes only, and so the views of the author should not be taken as expert instruction or commands. The reader is responsible for his or her own actions.

This book is not meant to be used, nor should it be used, to diagnose or treat any medical condition. For diagnosis or treatment of any medical problem, consult your own physician.

The people described in this book are real, but their names and circumstances have been changed to protect the confidentiality of each individual.

Neither the author nor the publisher assumes any responsibility or liability on behalf of the purchaser or reader of this book.

Buyer Bonus

As a way of saying thank you for your purchase, I'm offering a *free* download for my book readers.

I created a cheat sheet that will help you approach and talk to anybody.

>>> Go to www.socialconfidencemastery.com/cheatsheet

Inside, you will learn how to do the following:

- change your mindset by training your mind to improve the way you see yourself

- create a killer first impression and become a more likable person right away

- overcome social anxiety by building your courage to approach anybody you want to meet

- improve your conversation skills by learning how to tell good stories that captivate people

- design your ideal lifestyle by doing more of what you love while connecting with like-minded people

… and much, much more.

Dedication

This book is dedicated to all my previous students. You are the reason why I do what I do. I am honored to play a small role in your social success.

I also want to dedicate this book to my family, which has supported my unconventional journey thus far. Mom, Dad, Carlo, Jean—thank you for believing in me.

Let's not forget my friends who have inspired me to keep going during tough moments. Deon, Joe, Rachael, and Patrick—I'm grateful for your support.

Table of Contents

Chapter 1 - The Most Important Skill You Can Ever Learn 2

Chapter 2 - Where Shyness Comes From 8

Chapter 3 - Common Myths About Meeting New People 13

Chapter 4 - How to Become More Assertive 16

Chapter 5 - The New Psychology of Success 19

Chapter 6 - What to Do if You Feel Unlovable 24

Chapter 7 - How Social Media Lowers Your Self-Esteem 30

Chapter 8 - How to Stop Caring What People Think of You 35

Chapter 9 - How to Eliminate Fears That Hold You Back 39

Chapter 10 - Why Getting Rejected Is Actually a Good Thing 44

Chapter 11 - 7 Habits of Highly Irresistible Guys ... 47

Chapter 12 - How to Overcome Your Shyness Once and for All 53

Chapter 13 - The Best Way to Start a Conversation With Anybody 58

Chapter 14 - How to Motivate Yourself to Go Out . 61

Chapter 15 - How to Build a Quality Network 65

How to Use This Book

Here's the reality of your situation: anyone can pick up and read this book—but not everyone will see results.

The difference between the guy who improves his social confidence and the guy who just buys another book on social confidence is one simple thing: taking massive action.

If you want to get the most out of this book, I encourage you to do three things:

1. Have an open mind so you can accept new ideas.

2. Implement the strategies that you learn as you're reading.

3. Take what works and discard what doesn't.

These are the same steps that I took to change my own life and the lives of the clients I've worked with through my coaching program.

You can't just read a book and expect to get results. You need to apply what you learn consistently until it works for you.

That's why I've made this book actionable.

If you do this, I promise you that your personal, romantic, and professional lives will transform and you'll start becoming the man you've always wanted to be.

Chapter 1

The Most Important Skill You Can Ever Learn

I used to be terrified of talking to strangers.

A lot of people find that hard to believe just because they've seen me on television, heard me on the radio, or watched me speak on stage.

They often assume I've always been socially confident.

They think I always knew how to charm people and engage them in meaningful conversations. Or they think I've always been able to make friends on the spot and become the life of the party.

Wrong!

This couldn't be further from the truth.

My journey had very humble beginnings.

As an immigrant, I found it really challenging to fit in when my family moved to Canada from the Philippines when I was 16 years old.

My social anxiety back then was so bad that I can still remember eating my lunch in a bathroom stall back in high school. I was too terrified to mingle with the other kids, so I did everything I could to isolate myself.

In fact, I was so shy that I could barely hold eye contact with a girl that I was attracted to, or I'd stumble with my words whenever I would talk to someone who I thought was "cooler" than me.

I was paralyzed by fear, so in any social gathering, I would often be caught up in my own head while I watched everybody else have fun.

My career choice also didn't help my situation.

After I graduated from school, I got a job as a structural designer working for an engineering company. Even though it paid well, my work environment didn't promote a lot of social interactions.

I spent over eight hours every single working day looking at graphs, blueprints, and spreadsheets—not to mention the fact that I was usually surrounded by other socially awkward people. The only time we'd talk was when we had to ask each other something work-related.

Because I lacked the experience and skills to communicate my ideas effectively, I found it difficult to make friends, and I couldn't get a date to save my life.

This went on for years until I said enough was enough. I knew things had to change, except I had no idea where to start.

But I was persistent.

I knew that I had to find a way to get this part of my life handled or else I would end up depressed and desperate.

I wanted to feel in control of my ability to connect with people, and I was willing to do anything to make that happen.

After reading almost every book about social dynamics, studying under some of the best coaches in this industry, and experimenting on my own for many years, things finally started to make sense.

Contrary to what most people believe, having great social skills isn't just something you're born with; it's a learnable skill. It's no different than learning how to play a new instrument or a new sport

Knowing this gave me a lot of hope, and it made me persevere when things got tough in my journey. I knew that if I learned the right skill sets and kept practicing it over and over again, I could become confident, charismatic, and likable.

Looking back now, I wish I paid more attention to this part of my life rather than just getting good grades in school.

Nowadays, I realize that there's a direct correlation between your ability to create new relationships and your success in life.

Learning how to get along with people will do more for you than any fancy degree. Nobody cares about your GPA or how much money you make. But you need to have good social skills in order to make friends, get dates, and advance professionally.

Don't worry if you think you're someone shy. I was probably in a worse situation than you when I got started.

Trust me when I say that if I was able to overcome my social awkwardness, you can, too, with enough time, effort, and repetition.

The thing is, *who* you know matters more than *what* you know. If you lack social confidence, you're severely handicapping yourself in almost all aspects of your life.

That's why I wrote this book.

The lessons that I'm about to share with you are things that I wish I knew back then.

If you're someone who wants to succeed socially without being someone you're not, then this book is definitely for you. You'll discover how to build social confidence, no matter how shy you are.

Take one of my previous students, Henry, for example.

Henry worked for a tech company and made good money as a developer.

Despite his favorable financial situation, he was frustrated beyond belief because he didn't have the dating and social life that he wanted.

I can't really blame him, though. In fact, his story is very relatable to mine.

Like me, he believed that if he went to school, got good grades, and landed a great job, then everything else would take care of itself. He was raised by his parents to believe that academic success was his golden ticket in life.

I'm sure his parents had good intentions, and getting a good education is important. But in the grand scheme of things, that's only a small part of the equation.

During the coaching program, I helped Henry eliminate his negative self-talk, create a great first impression, and improve his conversation skills. We developed a plan that he could implement on a regular basis to create a thriving social life filled with quality relationships.

And because he took massive action consistently, it was no surprise that he was able to see such a drastic improvement in a short amount of time.

Last time I talked to him, he sounded a lot happier, and I could hear it in his voice.

He told me that he has fewer panic attacks, he's been going on more dates, and he regularly gets invited by friends to parties and fun events. Not only that, he's also moved up in his company to a management position.

Remember, all the money in the world is useless if you don't have anyone in your life to create memories with.

I promise that if you follow the advice I lay out in this book, you'll be able to build more confidence, overcome your social anxiety, and eliminate your insecurities.

Don't be that person who misses out on opportunities in life because you took too long to take action. You can't make more time, so be someone who quickly implements what they learn.

If you're ready to get this part of your life handled, then let's get started.

Chapter 2

Where Shyness Comes From

Being shy can hold you back from living a more fulfilling life.

Unlike introverts, who feel energized by time alone, shy people desperately want to connect with others. The only problem is, they don't know how or they can't tolerate the anxiety that comes with interacting with a total stranger.

Let's take Jim, one of my former students, as an example.

Jim works as an electrical engineer and was raised in a very religious family.

When he came to me for help, he told me how depressed he was, because he felt like he was missing out on so much that life had to offer. As a matter of fact, he'd never had a girlfriend and he had very few friends.

During the coaching program, he told me that it felt like there was a glass wall separating him from the people he wanted to interact with.

I relate to Jim so well because I understand exactly what he was going through.

I used to be someone who'd be stuck at home on Friday and Saturday nights. My phone never rang because I didn't have a lot of friends to go out with.

The odd time that I would go out or got invited to a party, I felt helpless and totally out of place. I was too nervous to walk up to people I wanted to meet, so I just kept to myself.

I became that guy who stood against the wall with my drink pressed against my chest, watching everybody else around me have a good time.

Can you relate to this?

If so, you're not alone. There's a solution to this problem, and that's what the rest of this book is all about.

But before we talk about how to overcome your shyness, you need to understand where it comes from first.

Here are a few potential sources of your shyness:

Source #1: Lack of Confidence

Understanding how to develop confidence is an integral part of succeeding socially.

According to Oxford dictionary, confidence is defined as "a feeling of self-assurance arising from one's appreciation of one's own abilities or qualities."

Developing confidence in any area of your life is really simple. All you have to do is learn pertinent skills on a particular subject and demonstrate competence in those skills over time.

That means you're going to have to go through a period where you suck at whatever you're learning before you get good at it.

Once you have enough reference experience from doing something repeatedly, that's when you gain confidence.

Confidence is domain-specific as well.

For example, just because you're confident at driving a car with an automatic transmission doesn't necessarily make you confident at driving a car with a manual transmission, because that requires a slightly different skill set.

So in this case, to become confident at meeting new people, all you have to do is learn the skills necessary to succeed socially and practice it over and over again.

Simply put, you just have to figure out what socially confident people do when they interact with others and become someone who has those traits.

Source #2: Not Feeling Good Enough

As a teenager, I was bullied a lot because I was overweight and had bad acne.

I used to weigh 200 pounds, I had a 36-inch waist, and my face resembled a slice of pepperoni pizza. My physical appearance made me feel self-conscious.

Today, I've managed to lose 60 pounds of fat, my skin is clearer, and I present myself well. But whenever I was reminded of that awkward time in my life, I would have feelings of inferiority.

I didn't know how to control my thoughts and I started to think that I was worthless, so I avoided getting close to other people.

Looking back now, I realize that my feelings of inferiority came from remembering past failures.

Later on in this book, I'll show you how to change your mindset and improve the way you see yourself.

Source #3: Perfectionism

Back in the day, I had an overwhelming desire to be liked by everybody.

Because I always wanted to say the right things, I became afraid of speaking up. And my social skills never improved because I never said anything.

I was stuck in a vicious circle.

If this sounds like you, I want you to understand that, in practice, there is no losing, only learning. Things are going to be messy sometimes, and that's okay.

The irony is, the less you care about making mistakes, the more socially confident you appear because you're just someone who speaks his mind.

To put things into perspective for you, there are billions of people in the world and there's no way you're going to get along with everybody. The sooner you can accept that, the faster you'll find people who like you for who you are.

Whether you can relate to some or all of the reasons where your shyness came from, no worries.

In the next few chapters, I'll be sharing with you some actionable steps to go from shy to social.

Chapter 3

Common Myths About Meeting New People

No matter how long you've been learning this stuff, there will always be some common myths that have been floating around and keeping shy guys lonely for ages.

I know this from experience.

In fact, I used to believe these myths, too. It wasn't until I realized that they weren't true that I was able to improve my situation.

Maybe it's that you have to go to the bar to meet people, or people will think you're weird if you approach them, or you don't have anything good to say.

Do any of those sound familiar?

If so, let's debunk these myths.

Myth #1: You Have to Go to the Bar to Meet People

I don't know about you, but I actually *hate* going to the bar.

But I still went because I thought I was supposed to.

Looking back now, I realize that the bar is probably the *worst* place for shy guys to meet people.

It's loud, it's expensive, and you're competing with other guys who are more outgoing than you.

So why make it hard when you can make it easier for yourself, right?

The best way to meet like-minded people is to go to places that are fun for you.

Find your passion, keep doing what you love, and invite people along the way.

Myth #2: People Will Think You're Weird

Walking up to someone you've never met before is something that people would probably label weird.

Why?

Because it falls outside the social norm.

But if you spend your life living inside the social norm, what kind of life do you think you'll end up with?

Boring, lame, and uninspiring.

That sucks more, doesn't it?

So do you want to be weird, or do you want to be happy?

The choice is yours.

Myth #3: You Have Nothing Good to Say

C'mon now!

That's impossible.

If you're in your 20s, you have at least a few decades of life experiences that you can talk about.

The reason why most guys feel paralyzed when it comes to meeting new people is because they want to come up with the "perfect thing" to say.

In reality, you can say whatever you want, as long as it matters to you.

Remember this: it's not about the moves you make; it's about making a move.

There you have it.

Don't let these myths hold you back from meeting new people and living the life you want.

Chapter 4

How to Become More Assertive

Because my family didn't have a lot of money when I was growing up, my dad had to work overseas to provide for us.

Even though it was something he had to do for us to survive, I unfortunately didn't have a strong male role model.

I didn't learn how to be a man, how to relate to other men, and how to behave around women.

It wasn't until later on in my life that I realized how this affected me in all my relationships. I became a people-pleaser and did everything I could so that others would approve of me.

In order to become more assertive, you have to learn how to stand up for what you believe in and ask for what you want.

Becoming the person you're meant to be means you are self-aware.

You have to understand who you are, what you want, and where you're going. Your thoughts, emotions, and actions are all in alignment. It's about living a life of purpose and positively impacting everyone you interact with.

Nowadays, it's difficult to get to know yourself.

We're bombarded with marketing messages from the media telling us who to be and how to act in order to fit in.

There's so much external noise that it's easy to forget to listen to what truly matters: your opinion of yourself.

If you want to become more assertive, you have to set very clear goals. When you're in complete alignment with who you are and what you want, there's no internal resistance. That's when you start to feel comfortable in your skin and you care a lot less about what people think of you.

The reason why most people don't get what they want is that they don't even know what it is to begin with.

If you're not sure what it is, here's what I suggest.

Take a bit of time to be quiet on a daily basis and ask yourself, "What do I want?"

Having a clearly defined goal acts like a filter because it helps you determine how to spend your time on a daily basis. It's easy to get what you want if you actually know what you're working toward.

We live in a society that keeps telling us what to do, so we've neglected our own wants and needs. That's why it's so important to regularly ask yourself that question until you get an answer.

Have you ever talked to someone who just loves their life and what they do?

It's very magnetic, isn't it?

If you want to become someone worth getting to know, you need to live a life of passion.

It's hard to be an interesting person if you don't live an interesting life. That's why, if you're not happy with your current situation, you have the choice and capability to change it. You are entirely up to you, and you can't blame other people for your outcome.

It's actually crazy, but a lot of my students in the past have told me that they actually found it difficult to figure out what they want.

That's why you have to be willing to put in the work that other people won't—so that you can live your life the way most people can't.

Chapter 5

The New Psychology of Success

Learning something new is always challenging.

I'm willing to bet that every single socially confident person you look up to didn't start off like that. At one point, they also had social anxiety.

Unfortunately, the majority of people quit when the going gets tough. What about those who persevered and actually transformed their lives? What do they all have in common?

According to Carol Dweck, in her book *Mindset*, how you think plays a major role in your learning and progress.

The view you adopt for yourself profoundly affects the decisions you make.

Your mindset will either limit your potential or enable your success. It's the difference between excellence and mediocrity. It influences your risk tolerance and your ability to face challenges.

Which mindset do you think you have?

Those with a growth mindset believe that abilities can be developed through dedication and hard work.

They are resilient and view learning as necessary for success. They know that they can change no matter what kind of person they think they are.

On the other hand, those with a fixed mindset believe that basic qualities like talents and intelligence are simply fixed traits.

Working hard at something means they're not meant to do it. Natural talent alone, without effort, will make them successful.

After learning about this, I became ecstatic. I began to view everything as a social experiment.

There was no failure, just unwanted results.

I knew that if I kept at it, I could be as confident, charming, and social as the other people I looked up to.

I realized that making a mistake is part of the process. Having awkward interactions is okay, and getting rejected is not to be taken personally.

Failure isn't a sign of inadequacy, just a lack of experience.

Having awareness about the different types of mindset is all you need to start making a change.

If that's not enough, here are the top benefits of adopting a growth mindset.

Benefit #1: You Enjoy Learning Something You're Not Good At

"If he can do it, I can do it, too." That's the attitude of someone with a growth mindset. Fear is replaced with curiosity.

It helps you love learning and continue to love it in the face of difficulties. You see mistakes and setbacks as a necessary part of the journey.

You're more focused on what you need to do instead of getting a result. Difficult situations become opportunities to grow, not threats to your identity.

Benefit #2: You Stop Comparing Yourself to Other People

The feeling of inadequacy has to be one of the most common issues I hear from my clients.

It's easy to feel this way when you're constantly looking at what other people are doing.

People with a growth mindset are focused on their own journey, not on others. They're thankful for everything they have, and that's why they're always happy.

Benefit #3: You Increase Your Resilience to Criticism

Having a growth mindset helps you welcome feedback. You begin to see criticism as a chance to improve.

A setback indicates that something didn't go as planned, and now you have the choice to do something different.

You can figure out what went wrong, learn from it, and prevent it from happening again.

Benefit #4: You Strengthen Your Self-Confidence

Self-confidence is the belief you have in your ability to get something done.

If you're not afraid of trying and making mistakes, you learn to trust yourself more and more.

Without a growth mindset, you'll throw in the towel before the fight even begins. Looking good becomes more important than learning.

Benefit #5: You Get Better at Taking Responsibility for Your Life

In the grand scheme of things, your life is entirely up to you. You are the common denominator in everything you do.

Those with a growth mindset take ownership for all their results, both good and bad. They're focused more on the solution than on the problem.

Also, know that you have both a growth and fixed mindset in different areas of your life.

The key is identifying when you're slipping into a fixed mindset and getting into a growth mindset as quickly as possible.

Imagine how different your life would be if you adopted a growth mindset more often.

What would you gain if you were willing to be uncomfortable more often?

Challenge yourself to be more mindful and adopt a growth mindset more regularly.

Chapter 6

What to Do if You Feel Unlovable

A lot of guys I've worked with fantasize about what it would be like to have close friends and a romantic partner treat them in a loving way.

What they don't realize is that they can give themselves the same feelings of love, understanding, and connection.

Before I learned that this was even possible, I made similar mistakes in all my past relationships.

I remember dating girls back in the day who made me feel less than who I am. I never felt loved, understood, or even appreciated, but I still stuck around until the inevitable breakup happened.

Looking back now, the only reason why I tolerated being in those relationships was because I almost felt like I deserved it. To tell you the truth, I didn't like who I was back then.

I used to put my happiness on other people because I never found it within myself. I was so afraid of being lonely that I kept jumping from one bad relationship to another because I couldn't stand being alone.

That's why, before you embark on your journey to build new relationships with other people, you need to have a good relationship with yourself first.

How you treat yourself will determine how other people treat you. That's when I realized that it's okay to be selfish.

When you take care of yourself and fill your own cup first, you can be fully present in all your interactions without needing anything from other people.

Treating yourself in a loving way allows you to get all your emotional needs met on your own.

This creates more satisfying, independent relationships with everyone you interact with rather than toxic, codependent relationships where it feels like you can't live without other people.

A lot of guys I've worked with shy away from this topic because they feel like it's unnecessary. They think that once they learn the tactics and strategies of how to approach people and say what they want, then all their problems with meeting people will magically go away.

But that's like putting a Band-Aid on a headache.

The reality is, once you improve the relationship you have with yourself, you automatically improve your relationships with others.

At the end of the day, it's never about what you say, but how you're saying it. And that comes down to your overall vibe as a person.

Here are my best tips if you feel like you're not lovable.

Tip #1: Change Your Dialogue

Most guys I've worked with have nasty self-talk.

They say things like, "You're such an idiot," "You messed it up again," and "You always make a fool out of yourself."

Do those sound familiar?

Now let me ask you this. If that's how you currently talk to yourself, would you still have friends if you talk to other people the same way?

Think about it. How would you talk to someone you care about?

You would be kind, compassionate, and encouraging, right?

That's why self-love starts with the way you talk to yourself. And it's as simple as speaking to yourself like how you would talk to a good friend.

Remember, what shows up in your mind also shows up in your body. You'll project exactly what you feel.

You can't hide your true feelings behind pickup lines and routines. In fact, it's going to do more harm than good in the long run because you're not learning how to manage your emotions.

If you don't like who you are, how can you expect other people to like you?

Your current situation reflects your current beliefs. If you have people in your life that make you feel like you're not good enough, it's because you do that to yourself first.

As soon as you start treating yourself in a more loving way, you'll stop putting up with negative behaviors from people.

Tip #2: Spend Time With Yourself

If you want to feel lovable, you need to show yourself what love is and what it feels like.

Implementing this is very simple. Make a list of things that you wish other people would do for you, and do it for yourself first.

For example, you can get a massage, you can take yourself out for a nice dinner, or you can go for a hike and spend time in nature.

Whatever it is, do little things every single day to show yourself that you matter. It doesn't have to be anything crazy extravagant as long as you're consistently paying attention to how you take care of yourself.

As I've mentioned earlier, if you like who you are, then you'll have other people treat you the same way. That's the difference between people respecting you and people treating you poorly.

Tip #3: Rediscover Your Passion

Henry David Thoreau once said, "Most men lead lives of quiet desperation and go to the grave with a song still in them."

This quote spoke to me, and that's why I decided to quit a job I hated and to go for the things that I wanted.

Remember, passion is sexy.

There's nothing more attractive than someone who lives their life the way they want to. Become that person.

If you're not sure where to start, simply define what your perfect day looks like.

Ask yourself what you would do. Where would you live? Who would you be spending time with?

Once you've taken the time to answer those questions, consciously align your actions to make that happen.

For me, I knew that I wanted to live a life of meaning and purpose. I wanted to earn a living in a way that serves other people, and I wanted to run my business from anywhere in the world.

After doing this exercise, it took me a few years to figure things out and carve my own path. But what's a few years in the grand scheme of things?

It's no surprise that today I'm living my perfect day, close to my original vision, because I was intentional about the actions I took.

If I'm presented with an opportunity that's not in alignment with the vision I have for my life, it's easy for me to say no. Having my perfect day mapped out also allows me to take action on the right things at the right time.

Find whatever it is you're excited to get out of bed for. That's when you'll transform yourself into the kind of person who attracts quality relationships in your life naturally.

Follow these tips on a daily basis and you'll attract amazing people in your life because you focused on the relationship that matters the most: the one with yourself.

Chapter 7

How Social Media Lowers Your Self-Esteem

There's no doubt.

Social media has become such an integral part of our lives.

For most people, it's the first thing they look at in the morning and the last thing they see at night.

Not that long ago, I left my phone at home by accident, and I remember feeling so much anxiety throughout the day. I felt so disconnected, like I was missing out on what everybody else was up to.

That's when I realized this was becoming an issue, because it was starting to affect how I felt personally.

I was so addicted to the attention I was getting on social media that I found it hard to be present with my friends and with what I was doing.

Don't get me wrong; I'm not saying social media is bad. Not at all.

It's one of the main tools I use to manage my business, keep in touch with my loved ones, and connect with people from different parts of the world.

At the same time, social media can negatively affect your social confidence if you're not aware of how to use it.

Here are the main reasons social media lowers your self-esteem.

Reason #1: It Creates Unrealistic Expectations

Have you ever scrolled through Instagram or Facebook, saw people you follow, and felt a little bit jealous?

They're usually dressed to the nines and look like they're just living it up.

Being exposed to these types of content regularly made me feel inadequate because I couldn't help but compare myself to them.

What I didn't realize was that all the images they posted were carefully curated and taken multiple times so that they looked just right.

Sometimes they're not even real.

The images people post online only show a small percentage of what their normal lives are actually like.

How do I know?

Because I've met these so-called social media influencers in real life, and they're no different than you and I.

They deal with their own fears and insecurities that they never talk about in public. Some of them even pretend to live a lifestyle that they can't afford.

That's why you shouldn't take anything you see online at face value.

People who are actually doing well in real life don't have time to post about it on social media.

Your goal is to be happy, not just look happy.

Reason #2: It Robs You of Your Ability to Be Present

I can't stand wasting my time.

That's why I get annoyed when I'm hanging out with people who are constantly on their phones. I was guilty of this, too, before I made a conscious decision to be more mindful and present.

If you want to improve the quality of your relationships, put your phone face-down the next time you're spending time with someone.

Another thing I suggest is to go through your phone settings and turn off your notifications. Allocate time throughout the day to catch up with everyone on social media, and then go live your life.

Pay more attention to whomever you're with than to your social media friend count and followers. Your fear of missing out online is causing you to actually miss out in real life.

Reason #3: It Creates Analysis Paralysis

A lot of students I've worked with have told me they feel overwhelmed with the amount of information available online.

Some of them would just sit at home, scrolling through their newsfeeds and clicking on different links.

The next thing they know, they're watching hours and hours of videos on YouTube, reading articles on different websites, and feeling like they're getting things done.

But when it's time to actually implement what they learned, they feel paralyzed because there are so many things going on in their heads.

Being busy isn't the same as being productive.

If you want to prevent this from happening to you, make it a point to only take in information for what you need at that moment.

A good rule of thumb is to spend twice as much time implementing something as you did learning it. If you spent an hour of reading, take action for at least two hours before you read anything else.

As mentioned before, I'm not saying social media is bad. But you have to make sure you're using it for what it's designed for: enhancing your relationships with the people who matter to you.

Chapter 8

How to Stop Caring What People Think of You

There's a comfort zone challenge popularized by Tim Gross from Comfort Zone Crusher that's meant to overcome social anxiety.

Basically, you would lie down in the middle of a crowded public place, remain silent on the ground for about 10 seconds, and then get up and go on with your day.

It sounded simple, but when I actually did it, it was definitely not easy.

One day, I decided to lie down in the middle of a busy mall, and to be honest with you, I wanted to crawl out of my own skin while I was doing this comfort zone challenge. I thought people would make fun of me and think I was weird.

But while I was lying on my back, I looked around and noticed something interesting.

Nobody cared.

There were a few people that gave me funny looks, but most of them just walked past me.

That's why I think it's a good idea to do something that scares you as often as you can. Eventually, you'll learn how to get comfortable being uncomfortable.

That's the whole idea behind exposure therapy. If you keep doing the things that scare you, eventually they no longer will.

This actually reminds me of Riley, one of my previous coaching clients.

When Riley reached out to me for help, he was very self-conscious. I found his situation interesting because he's a tall, attractive, and well-spoken guy.

But the thing holding him back from putting himself out there was that he cared way too much what other people thought of him. This made him paranoid, and he would overanalyze every single interaction that he had.

When we worked together, he would bring up these small day-to-day scenarios and blow them out of proportion. He was always thinking what people meant when they said or did something.

You can see how this way of thinking will cause anyone to be socially anxious, right?

After Riley followed the advice I'm about to share with you, he was able to control his thoughts, quiet that negative voice in his head, and feel more relaxed in any social setting.

If you want to stop caring what people think of you, here are my best tips.

Tip #1: Meditate Daily

Adding a meditation practice to my morning routine has to be one of the best things I've ever done.

I started just by closing my eyes and focusing on my breathing for a few minutes a day, and it has made a huge difference in my life.

Meditation trains your mind to create space between you and your thoughts. From then on, you can identify which ones you want to keep and which ones you want to get rid of.

Tip #2: Visualize Success

Your mind doesn't know the difference between perception and reality.

If you don't believe me, picture yourself biting through a wedge of lime. If you imagined it clearly enough, your mouth will begin to salivate.

The same thing happens when you feel anxiety by worrying about your situation. Your mind is coming up with mental images of what you perceive to be the worst-case scenario.

If you want to program your mind to succeed, simply imagine what your desired outcome would look like, and train yourself to entertain that idea instead.

Tip #3: Don't Take Things Personally

You have no idea what's going on in people's lives.

Most of them have their own personal issues they're dealing with. How they react at any moment has nothing to do with you.

The best thing you can do is to give everyone the benefit of the doubt. Believe that people have good intentions until proven otherwise.

Adopt this mindset and you won't feel offended as easily.

Follow these tips if you want to feel less socially anxious and express yourself fully in any situation.

Chapter 9

How to Eliminate Fears That Hold You Back

According to Oxford dictionary, fear is an unpleasant emotion caused by the belief that someone or something is dangerous and likely to cause pain or threat.

What that means is that it's all in your head.

As mentioned earlier, fear is caused by the interpretation you give to your situation, which gives you a negative emotion.

For example, let's say you're at a party and you want to approach a group of people.

If you think they're not going to like you, you will start to feel the pain of rejection, as if the group already turned you down.

The opposite is also true.

If you assume that they're going to welcome you, then you will subconsciously behave in a way that makes you come across as someone worth getting to know.

When you change the story you tell yourself, you change how you feel, which causes you to do something different.

It's that simple.

Despite what you're afraid of, I want to share with you a simple process that will help you eliminate fears that hold you back.

Step #1: Identify the Fear

It's human nature to fear the unknown. That's why the first step to overcoming fear is to define the things that scare you.

Ask yourself what fears hold you back from getting the relationships you want in your life.

Once you have them written down, you can think about them strategically.

Here's an example.

Let's say one of the fears you wrote down is that you'll run out of things to say when you approach a group of people you want to meet.

Step #2: Visualize the Fear

Logic alone doesn't remove fear. To overcome it effectively, you have to allow yourself to process the emotions that it brings.

You can do this by asking yourself what the best- and worst-case scenarios are.

By having an understanding of everything that can potentially happen, making decisions about how to deal with it becomes easier.

Going back to your fear of running out of things to say, the worst-case scenario is that you have an awkward silence in your conversation.

Big deal, right?

The best-case scenario is that the group finds you interesting and invites you to the next party.

Step #3: Destroy Fear with Preparation

It's easy to feel scared when you don't know what to expect.

Whatever you're afraid of, you can always take an active role to do something about it.

Go back to your list of fears and begin to fill in knowledge gaps.

You can replace fear with excitement by asking questions and doing research.

If not knowing what to say is something you struggle with, what can you do to prepare for it?

Well, you can come up with some interesting things to talk about ahead of time. You can also take an improv class or sign up for a public speaking class.

As you can see, coming up with solutions is just as easy as coming up with excuses.

Step #4: Consider the Cost of Keeping the Fear

Fear has its uses. It's kept you alive so far, right?

But the cost of holding on to it is sometimes greater.

What is the risk of not taking action?

Well, it's costing you time, which is your most valuable resource because you can't make more of it.

It's costing you energy because this is probably something you think about all the time.

More importantly, it's costing you your happiness. Because you're not taking action, you've missed out on so many great interactions that you could've had.

You have two options.

You can take the risk that the worst-case scenario might happen, or you can guarantee that you're going to keep enduring the pain of your current situation.

The choice is yours.

Step #5: Define the Next Action

Confidence is a by-product of the actions you take. If you want to overcome fear, don't just sit around and do nothing.

Get out there and get busy.

Since you spend a lot of time thinking about what scares you, avoiding fear is actually more energy intensive than just dealing with it.

Ask yourself what you can do in the next 20 minutes to take a small step toward the fear.

To continue on with our example of improving your conversation skills, maybe start doing research on a class you want to take.

Put it in your calendar and commit to doing it.

There you have it. This is the same process I go through when I'm afraid of something, and this is the same exercise I teach my coaching clients. I encourage you to give it a shot if you want to overcome any fear that holds you back from going for what you want.

Chapter 10

Why Getting Rejected Is Actually a Good Thing

Building up the courage to walk up to someone you want to talk to is hard enough. Getting rejected is even harder.

Rejection hurts because it triggers the same part of your brain as when you experience physical pain.

That's why it feels like you got stabbed by a sharp knife and someone's twisting it.

But here's the thing: rejection is not about you. As a matter of fact, it's selfish to think that way.

The reason why you can't take rejection personally is because you have no idea what people are going through when you interact with them.

Maybe their boss yelled at them at work. Maybe they're having relationship issues. Or maybe they're just having a bad day.

Who knows?

You can't know what's going on in peoples' heads. But if you're going to make up stuff in your head to explain what happened, why not give it a positive interpretation?

It's all in your mind anyway. You can believe anything you want, so you might as well fill your head with more empowering thoughts.

Personally, I would rather take the risk and go for what I want than live a life of regrets and always think of what could've happened.

Also, you'll meet three different types of people in any given situation.

The first type you'll meet are people who are not interested in meeting you because they're in a rush or they're in a bad mood.

The second type are people who are indifferent about meeting you, and the conversation can go either way.

And lastly, the third type are people who are interested in meeting you, and they're open to hearing what you have to say.

What does this mean for you?

The reason why getting rejected is actually a good thing is because it saves you from wasting time with the wrong people.

Your job is to filter out those who are not a good fit for you as quickly as possible and move on.

Give yourself the opportunity to meet people who will like you for who you are.

The best thing you can do when you get rejected is to recognize it, accept it, and keep going anyway.

Chapter 11

7 Habits of Highly Irresistible Guys

I mean, c'mon.

Who doesn't want to become highly irresistible?

Back in the day, I was always jealous of guys who seemed to have "it."

They're confident, social, and charismatic. Men respect them, and women love them.

I was in desperate need to figure this out because I was so tired of being socially awkward.

That's why I made it a priority to study the most socially confident guys out there. I went out of my way to meet them at events and conferences, interview them on my podcast, and build relationships with them. After many years of doing that, I eventually saw a pattern.

Curious to know what those are?

Here are seven habits of highly irresistible guys.

Habit #1: They Like Themselves

Like what I said earlier, self-love is the most important thing you need to learn in order to become irresistible.

How other people treat you is a reflection of how you treat yourself. This is so important it's worth repeating.

If others aren't responding well to you, it's because you're encouraging that kind of behavior around you.

Back in the day, I felt like I wasn't good enough. Because of that feeling, I'd let people around me treat me poorly.

The opposite is also true.

If you like who you are, then you will not tolerate any bullshit from other people.

You need to see yourself as someone worthwhile if you want your relationships to change for the better.

Remember, you'll get exactly what you think you deserve.

Habit #2: They Present Themselves Well

Let's be honest: looks are important.

First impressions make a huge difference on how people perceive you because we make snap judgments about others right away. We're always sizing up everyone we meet, trying to figure out if they're a friend or a foe. That's just how we're wired.

If you want to become highly irresistible, you have to pay attention to how you're coming across.

By taking care of your style and grooming, every aspect of your life will improve. Not only will you look more confident, but you'll also feel more confident, which can lead to more romantic and professional opportunities.

Habit #3: They Make Others Feel Important

Highly irresistible guys are good listeners and ask good questions.

They're secure enough with themselves that they don't feel the need to brag or one-up whomever they're talking to. They're comfortable in their own skin, and they have nothing to prove.

That's why other people feel understood while in their presence.

Keep in mind that every single person you interact with has a story to tell, so be curious and have a genuine desire to get to know them.

Habit #4: They Are Courageous

Nothing good ever comes from playing it safe, and socially confident guys know this.

They handle rejection well because they know that they have no control over how other people are going to react to them.

That's why they're only focused on things they can do something about, like the actions they take and the interpretation they give to any situation.

I encourage you to always put yourself out there and go for what you want. The more you do this, the more you'll respect yourself because you're acting on things that are important to you.

Remember, courage isn't the absence of fear but your willingness to act regardless of how you feel.

Habit #5: They Are Authentic

Have you ever noticed that the harder you try to be impressive in conversation, the more it backfires on you?

Funny how that works, huh?

Highly irresistible guys don't hide their emotions, and they just say what's on their minds. Because they have a positive self-image, they feel good about who they are, so they're not afraid to be seen.

That's why learning how to become more vulnerable is so important. By sharing your flaws and your struggles, you become a lot more relatable to everyone you talk to.

Habit #6: They Are Optimistic

There are always two sides to every story: the good and the bad.

Why not choose the one that will benefit you the most?

Highly irresistible guys always find the lesson in every situation. If an interaction doesn't go as planned, they reflect on what they could've done better, but they don't beat themselves up over it.

Also, positivity is very attractive. Don't be surprised if you find more solutions than problems when you are optimistic.

You'll get exactly what you're looking for, so train your mind to see the good in every situation.

Habit #7: They Are Passionate

Highly irresistible guys love what they do. And because they enjoy it, they eventually become really good at it.

This point is so important that you'll hear me mention this throughout this book. You were not put on this planet to just exist, so stop wasting your time doing something you hate.

Personally, ever since I stopped doing anything that didn't make me happy, my life became more meaningful and exciting.

You owe it to yourself to find what you're passionate about and do more of what you love.

If you're not sure where to start, just ask yourself what you would do if money wasn't an issue. Give that some thought and go from there. The more action you take, the more the right path will reveal itself.

There you have it. Now you know the habits that I've observed from highly irresistible guys. I can promise you that if you follow these tips, you, too, will become highly irresistible.

Chapter 12

How to Overcome Your Shyness Once and for All

Earlier in the book, we talked about where your shyness could potentially come from.

If you lack confidence, you don't feel good enough, or you suffer from perfectionism, there is a simple process that you can implement to overcome your shyness.

Let's take Jerry, a previous student, for example.

His parents were from Vietnam, and he was raised in Texas, where he was perceived to be different than everybody else.

Because he didn't feel like he fit in, he grew up very quiet and reserved. His parents pushed him to be the best he could be in school, but they would always punish him whenever he made mistakes.

Jerry spent so much time studying and pleasing other people that it's no surprise he became timid. He didn't have a lot of friends, and he always got taken advantage of by almost every girl he dated.

When he came to me for help, he wanted to control the types of relationships in his life rather than settling for what was available.

If you can relate to his story, I want to share a few things that have helped him during the coaching program.

Here are my best tips to help you overcome your shyness.

Tip #1: Set Small Goals

Trying to do too many things at once can feel overwhelming. When you're just starting out, keep things as simple as possible.

I suggest you take the time to learn the fundamentals first.

When you're starting out, set a goal to just get good at making eye contact and smiling at strangers.

Once you're comfortable doing that, say hello and ask them how their day is going. After that, see if you can hold a conversation for a few minutes.

That's when you can add a bit of humor or a bit of flirting. But before you get there, you need to be able to start holding a conversation first.

Do you see where I'm going with this?

The key here is to learn things systematically. Lower the bar and manage your expectations.

Get into the habit of feeling like you're always winning, because nothing builds social confidence faster than seeing results.

Tip #2: Improve Gradually

The only way you'll get better is by continuously being challenged.

That's why you need to always take risks and work on expressing your true personality in every situation. Doing small talk is fine, but don't be afraid to voice your opinion and share what matters to you.

Whatever you're into, do your best to bring up topics that are important to you in every conversation. People will either resonate with you or they won't. Either way is fine.

The more authentic you are, the faster you'll meet other like-minded people.

Tip #3: Get Feedback

It's hard to improve if you don't know exactly what to work on.

That's why having someone show you your blind spots is critical.

Ask people you know, like, and trust to give you feedback about how they see you and what you could do better.

Get them to tell you your strengths and weaknesses.

Better yet, work with a coach that you trust and respect. My results skyrocketed when I decided to just ask for help and work with someone who knows what they're doing.

For me, one of the many valuable insights I received was that I used to talk way too fast and I would ask way too many questions.

Yeah, it sucked, but it was what I needed to hear.

Whatever feedback you get, don't take it personally. Learn from it and use it to improve your interactions in the future.

By doing this, you'll get a better understanding of yourself, how you appear to others, and what you can do better.

Tip #4: Find Socially Skilled People

Reading books on social confidence (like this one) is totally fine, but you'll learn a lot faster by seeing someone who's actually socially confident interact with other people in person.

Once you find socially skilled people, observe their mindset and behaviors. Pay close attention to what they're doing and find ways to make it your own.

Remember, your environment shapes how you turn out, so be aware of who you spend time with.

Tip #5: Stay Consistent

Small actions performed repeatedly produce massive results.

As mentioned earlier, by talking and connecting with new people consistently, you'll develop your social confidence muscle.

The opposite is also true. If you don't make time to go out and socialize, it's easy to fall back into your old habits.

It's no different than going to the gym. If you don't work out, your body will eventually atrophy.

The more experience you acquire, the more you'll find yourself feeling confident in any social setting.

Eventually, connecting with other people will become a habit and you'll begin to notice a wider range of opportunities in your life.

Don't be deceived by how simple these tips are. At the end of the day, the best plan for you is the one that you can actually implement.

Try these tips out, and let me know how it goes.

In the next chapter, I'll teach you a dead simple way to start a conversation with anybody. It's virtually guaranteed to work in any situation.

Chapter 13

The Best Way to Start a Conversation With Anybody

Would you like to know the *best* way to start a conversation with someone?

Before I tell you what it is, I want to share something personal with you.

I used to overcomplicate this process.

For example, if I saw a cute girl that I wanted to meet, I would pace back and forth in my head, trying to come up with something witty to say.

This would go on for a few minutes, and by the time I'd mustered up the courage to say something, it was too late.

She'd already walked too far away, and I was left admiring her from a distance.

Once again, I was kicking myself for not taking action.

If that sounds familiar to you, don't worry. There's an easier way to start a conversation with someone you want to meet.

In fact, this strategy is so effective that you can use it anytime, anywhere, and on anyone.

Not only that, but it's virtually impossible to come across as weird or creepy if you do this correctly.

Curious to know what it is? Here it is.

Walking up to someone and giving them a genuine compliment is the *best* way to start a conversation.

Why is that?

Because you're giving value instead of taking value.

Think about that for a moment. Imagine how nice it feels to hear kind words from someone you don't know.

Your conversation could be something like this.

"You have good style. What do you do for work?"

"That's a cool leather jacket. Where did you buy it from?"

"You seem fit. What sport do you play?"

Adding a question in the end also gives the other person an opportunity to respond to your compliment.

If you want to continue the conversation, you can introduce yourself by saying your name, or you can just end it there. Either way, you just made someone's day.

Isn't that awesome?

Personally, in a variety of social settings, I've met people with great success just by giving them a genuine compliment. I've done this while sitting in coffee shops, working out at the gym, or eating dinner at a restaurant.

You can't go wrong by making other people feel good about themselves. A genuine compliment is always a step in the right direction to becoming more social.

The key here is to train yourself to look for what's good about people. There's always something about them that you can comment on. Also, the more specific the compliment is, the better.

Do this enough, and you'll eventually build a better social life full of genuine connections without being someone you're not.

Chapter 14

How to Motivate Yourself to Go Out

I get it.

Meeting new people is a huge struggle, especially if you're shy.

It's hard to keep doing something if you're not initially good at it, right?

Before I learned how to be socially confident, I spent a lot of time in isolation. Trust me, it wasn't because I didn't want to go out; I just had nobody to go out with, and it sucked.

Back then, I would rather jump out of a plane without a parachute than go out and meet new people.

Okay, maybe not. But you get the point.

This reminds me of Ivan, one of my previous coaching clients.

Ivan worked for an engineering company and was terribly shy. He had bad social anxiety and easily got overwhelmed when there were too many people around him.

Even though he was good-looking and made a decent living, he barely had friends and didn't have a lot of success with his romantic relationships.

When we started working together, I asked him how often he went out. He said he barely did because he thought his only option was to go to bars and clubs, which he absolutely hated.

During the coaching program, I helped him find venues that were more in alignment with his core values. This made socializing way more enjoyable for him.

As of when we last chatted, he's made some good friends and now actively goes on dates with women that he's interested in.

I'm about to share with you exactly how he did it.

Here are my best tips to help you out.

Tip #1: Prepare in Advance

If going out feels like a chore for you, then you're doing it all wrong.

As mentioned earlier, do a bit of research and go to events that you actually enjoy.

Take the time to come up with a few default icebreakers and stories you want to share in the conversation.

Once you have a handful of great interactions under your belt, you're going to feel more comfortable about your ability to approach and meet new people.

Preparation breeds confidence. Once you're there, you can enjoy yourself more because you came ready.

Tip #2: Set Yourself Up to Win

Learning something new is always challenging.

That's why you need to build positive momentum by finding the easiest thing you can do first.

Make sure the goals you set when you go out are challenging but still attainable.

It doesn't matter if you're working on holding better eye contact, saying hello to strangers, or starting to engage them in small talk.

As mentioned earlier, the key is to manage your expectations and celebrate what's working well. Look for every excuse to tell yourself you're doing a great job.

Nothing feels better than success. By focusing on small wins, you'll be more encouraged to keep going.

Tip #3: Love the Process

Everything takes time, so be easy on yourself.

If you've been struggling socially for many years, you can't expect to figure this out overnight.

As long as you have a plan that you're following and you're doing what you can, then you're on the right path.

Let's take my fitness journey, for example.

Back in the day, I was 60 pounds overweight. I wanted to get abs so badly that I actually developed an eating disorder.

It wasn't until I learned to love the process of eating healthy and going to the gym that I lost weight. Because I didn't take a shortcut, I was able to develop the right habits and keep the weight off—even until today.

Improving your social confidence is no different. Until you learn how to love the process of interacting with people for the sake of it, it's always going to be an uphill battle for you.

Remember, who you become matters more than what you do.

Keep these tips in mind next time you're stuck and don't feel like going out.

Chapter 15

How to Build a Quality Network

It's no secret.

If you want to create unlimited opportunities for yourself, you need to master the art of building a quality network.

Whether you're looking for a new job, a recommendation, or just someone to hang out with, you reach out to people that you know first.

That's why you have to be deliberate about growing your social circle. The bigger your network is, the more fulfilling your life is going to be.

If you want to be able to successfully build a social circle from scratch, here are my best tips.

Tip #1: Define What Matters to You

Mutual interest is the foundation of any great relationship.

It's so much easier to spend time with someone if both of you have lots of things in common.

Before you build your social circle, you have to get clear about what type of people you want to meet.

Take a moment and define your values. What are the things that are important to you?

For example, I wanted to be surrounded by positive and highly motivated individuals, so networking with other influencers and entrepreneurs was a big priority for me.

Remember, you become the average of the people you spend the most time with. You have to be intentional about whom you keep close to you because your environment shapes who you are.

Tip #2: Show Up at the Right Place

Now that you're clear about the type of people you want to meet, where do you think they hang out?

This could be both offline and online.

Start by finding relevant events in your city and being part of communities on your preferred social networking platforms. Show up there every day, provide value, and engage with the other members.

For example, whenever I move to a new city, I spend a lot of time at trendy coffee shops, coworking spaces, and personal development seminars. Why? Because I knew the type of people I wanted to meet would be there.

I also joined some relevant Facebook groups and started getting to know other members who were there, so I'm almost guaranteed to know someone who knows people in every city that I go to.

Tip #3: Organize Your Own Events

Remember, the host of the party has the highest social value, and you want to become that person.

People want to meet other like-minded people, so take the initiative and bring everyone cool and interesting you've met together. Organizing your own event doesn't have to be anything complicated. It could be as simple as just hosting a dinner party.

For example, I would organize a get-together at a restaurant where I would invite everyone I met throughout the week, and I would also encourage them to invite their friends.

This is one of the main strategies I've used to grow my social circle in a very short amount of time.

Be a good host and ensure you make everyone feel welcome. Mention something interesting when you introduce people to each other so they have something to work with.

The key here is to leverage your connections.

Tip #4: Provide Massive Value

Nobody has it all figured out.

It doesn't matter who you are and what you do; people are always struggling with something.

That's why you want to be the ultimate connector.

For example, if you know someone who needs a website and you know a good web developer, introduce them to one another. If you know someone who's struggling with their weight and you know a good personal trainer, put them in touch with each other.

Heck, if you have a single friend and you know someone whom they'd get along with, be their matchmaker!

Pair people up based on what they have and what they need.

Tip #5: Be Thoughtful

Do you know someone who only reaches out to you when they need something?

It's annoying, isn't it? So don't be that person.

Great relationships develop organically and happen over a period of time.

Take a moment out of your day to reach out to someone and just see how they're doing.

I would usually text my friends and mention that I was thinking about them and that I wanted to see how they're doing. I also call people whom I haven't spoken to in a while.

Thoughtfulness does go a long way, and by the time you need something, you have people in your network who have your back.

Keep these tips in mind, and you'll be able to build a quality network in no time at all.

Final Thoughts

By reading this book, you now have a plan to improve your social confidence.

If you follow what I've laid out in this book, you will transform your personal, romantic, and professional life—I guarantee it.

I wrote this book because I wanted to share the process of going from shy to social so that you don't experience all the mistakes I made early on.

It's basically bulletproof.

The next step is up to you.

The key is to take action: take the first step and begin the process of improving your social confidence.

Make a commitment to yourself.

You may have some awkward moments. You may experience a few painful rejections.

But the benefits of having effective communication skills outweigh the small discomfort you may temporarily endure.

I am sharing my system through this book to help shy guys create a life of design, not by default.

You picked up this book for a reason.

It sparked your interest because you never want to feel lonely again. Whatever your motivation is, you took the first step.

Although you have everything you need to get this part of your life handled, you may be looking for more help.

I encourage you to check out my coaching program. I promise it will be the best investment you ever make in yourself.

The program will give you in-depth information, fast-action guides, and step-by-step instructions that are impossible to include in a single book.

If you're serious about improving your social confidence, this program will help you get results.

If you're interested in the program, take a moment to book your free consultation by filling out an application form.

>>> Go to
www.socialconfidencemastery.com/consultation

Regardless of whether you join the program or not, I want to hear your success stories.

I hope you send me a message telling me how you are doing and how your life has changed as a result of improving your social confidence.

You can reach me at
info@socialconfidencemastery.com.

Here's to your social success.

Myke Macapinlac

Your Next Step

I'm confident that you now have the plan to improve your social confidence.

But here's the thing.

In order to take the next step, you need to know how to apply this to your day-to-day life.

That's why I created a cheat sheet that will help you approach and talk to anybody no matter how shy you are.

>>> Go to www.socialconfidencemastery.com/cheatsheet

Inside, you will learn how to do the following:

- change your mindset by training your mind to improve the way you see yourself

- create a killer first impression and become a more likable person right away

- overcome social anxiety by building your courage to approach anybody you want to meet

- improve your conversation skills by learning how to tell good stories that captivate people

- design your ideal lifestyle by doing more of what you love while connecting with like-minded people

… and much, much more.

Check Out My Other Books

Would you like to learn how to improve your confidence, charisma, and social skills?

If so, I've written other books that will make you successful in all your social interactions.

>>> Go to www.socialconfidencemastery.com/books

You'll improve your social skills faster, meet the type of people you want to meet, and build the lifestyle you've always dreamed of.

Take action today and get this part of your life handled once and for all.

Can You Do Me a Favor?

Thanks for checking out my book.

I'm confident you will improve your social confidence if you follow what's written inside. But before you go, I have one small favor to ask.

Would you take 60 seconds and write a quick blurb about this book on Amazon?

Reviews are the best way for independent authors (like me) to get noticed, sell more books, and spread their messages to as many people as possible.

I also read every review and use the feedback to write future revisions—and even future books.

Please manually navigate to the book's page on Amazon in order to leave a review.

Thank you—I really appreciate your support.

Printed in Great Britain
by Amazon

About the Author

Myke Macapinlac was a shy immigrant who used to work a boring engineering job and became a talk show host, a social dynamics specialist, and a lifestyle entrepreneur.

He now teaches shy guys to develop social confidence so they can succeed in their personal, romantic, and professional lives.

His work has been featured in the *Calgary Herald*, on *Breakfast Television*, on Shaw TV, and in the *Huffington Post*.

To get to know him personally, visit his website at www.socialconfidencemastery.com